Pip's pizza

Story written by Gill Munton
Illustrated by Tim Archbold

Speed Sounds

Consonants

Ask children to say the sounds.

f	l	m	n	r	s	v	z	**sh**	**th**	ng
ff	**ll**		nn			ve	**zz**			**nk**
							s			

b	c	d	g	h	j	p	qu	t	w	x	y	ch
bb	k		**gg**					tt	wh			tch
	ck											

Each box contains one sound but sometimes more than one grapheme.
Focus graphemes for this story are ***circled****.*

Vowels

Ask children to say the sounds in and out of order.

a	e	i	o	u
at	h**e**n	**i**n	**o**n	**u**p

ay	ee	igh	ow	oo
d**ay**	s**ee**	h**igh**	bl**ow**	z**oo**

Story Green Words

Ask children to read the words first in Fred Talk and then say the word.

Zip Pip yum smell tum egg jam thank

Ask children to say the syllables and then read the whole word.

pizz|a

Ask children to read the root first and then the whole word with the suffix.

rub → rubbed nut → nuts

Red Words

Ask children to practise reading the words across the rows, down the columns and in and out of order clearly and quickly.

I	said	the
he	no	you
your	be	are
my	of	put

Pip's pizza

"Yum, yum!" said Zip.

"I can smell pizza!"

Zip rubbed his tum.

Pip put nuts
on the pizza.

He put an egg
on the pizza.

Then he put red jam
on the pizza!

He put fish
on the pizza!

"Hot pizza!" said Pip.

He cut the pizza up.

“This bit is Zip’s,” he said.

“No, thank you!” said Zip.

Questions to talk about

Ask children to TTYP for each question using 'Fastest finger' (FF) or 'Have a think' (HaT).

p.8	(FF)	What did Zip say?
pp.10–11	(FF)	What did Pip put on the pizza?
p.12	(HaT)	Why did Pip need to be careful with the pizza?
p.13	(FF)	What did Zip say when he was offered the pizza?